The Red Rubber Ball
of Happiness

T0158570

For Ruby and Eddy
(when you're old enough)

Frances Williams
The Red Rubber Ball of Happiness

seren

Seren is the book imprint of
Poetry Wales Press Ltd
Nolton Street, Bridgend, Wales
www.seren-books.com

ISBN 1-85411-336-4

A CIP record for this title is available from the British Library.

The publisher acknowledges the financial assistance
of the Welsh Books Council.

Printed by Dinefwr Press, Llandybie.

Cover photograph by Alan Williams.

Contents

The Boy and the Balloon

after René Magritte

Two events shaped him.
The first was the strange arrival
On a summer's day
Of a huge and hovering
Hot air balloon. It landed
So softly on the roof,
Holding two men in the basket,
Hissing with secrets
And loaded with sand.
The second was the death
Of his mother. In the air
Was where exchange was made:
Chance for certainty,
Heaviness of grief
For lightness of belief,
A foolery of hats, pipes and papas.

He weighed up her body
Next to the magic
Of the pink and sinking sun.

What was to become of him
Then became inevitable: the apple
In his hand swelling to the size
Of the living room's dimension,
Its woody fragrance
Thick in his lungs
Like a green gas.

How big can ever a mother be?
Was the question he asked
As he pulled up the sheet
To the edge of his head
Cutting it off from his neck
Completely. How the night then

Would cover him,
With its mottled skin,
With its latticed scenery
In snowflakes down the corridor,
Treading so lightly you would not know
The world had come and gone again.

Learning Numbers by Heart

We hail the taxi in the nick of time,
Spotted with the first big splats,
The drummer on the roof
Alarming you. Lightning,
Thin as a blink,
And I count the seconds
Till the thunder comes,
Measuring the gap: close
And getting closer. In the park,
Under the wide and dripping trees,
Men stand like sentries or the dead,
Wearing balefulness
And making do
With caps of newsprint.
Mothers make a dash for it
As gutters grow ravenous
And gleefully we see
Our wings of water
Spray the ankles
Of every unfortunate.

You grip tighter onto me
And talk about the monster
In the puppet show we saw,
The one who had a face
Like a beast. But he was a man
Underneath. Just a grown-up man
Behind the painted mask....

Through the window's weeping,
I see you living on ahead of me
And wonder if there'll always be
This bit of you

Afraid of the storm
In the backseat of a cab,
Leather bound, mystic,
Listening to The Delphonics
With the casual driver
Tapping his finger on the wheel
To the chorus line:
'Didn't I do it this time, didn't I?'

We count our blessings,
Arrive back at your home just as
The minims drop their lines.
The storm is stopping.
The tarmac shines for miles.

The Snow Collector

after Wilson 'Snowflake' Bently, the first
man to photograph a snow crystal

Hexagonal vexations –
Bursting arms of thorny beauty –
Their detailed story
Blown at odds
Within the miraculous
Collections of vast
Piled-up indifference.
But he looked first:

I can't remember when
I didn't love the snow
More than anything
Except my mother.

Winter saw his range
Of focus dotted
In the intricate
Micrographic locus
Of true originality.
Each one was its
Own master and
Held a single clue.

There really wasn't much that he
Could add to that, except pursue
His line of blind obsession:
In forty-seven years of study
He collected and observed
Five thousand, three hundred
And eighty one variations
On the theme of snow.

Where the snowflake blew
He could also be found, stooping
Down to pick up off the ground
Handfuls of treasure. Some
Came to rest upon
The shelving of his Trilby hat,
Lacing his attention with little ironies –
Additions to his person
That he could not see,
Nor stop to measure,
Meltings in the realm of pure
Snowflake pleasure.

Signals

A bird is keeping you awake,
Peeping a line of eerie sharps
At eight o'clock, insistent in a tree.
He is saying goodnight, I venture
As I pull the duvet to your chin,
To all the little children in his nest.
You test my theory slowly
In the muscles of your brow.
I kiss your cheek,
Smooth as the roses that
Loosen their fists of perfume
To fall down piece by piece
Onto the lawn. But just as

I reach the door, you ask again
Then why is he saying it so often?
A bird sings only songs,
And so it's never wrong
To say the same thing twice,
I answer, in league
With the treacherous cat
Who leaps now, over the wall.
You gaze out of the window,
Its remedies of dark,
The bird heard
But not seen
Feathering your mind.

When I check on you
A little later, you are
Fast asleep, upside down
With arms outstretched
Miming a migration of your own.
You semaphore right through the night
With heavy, twitching hands,
As all the world in flight purports to land.

The Teenager Trees

Through the gaps we see
The children perform
Their parents
– miniature and true –
Mimics who'll grow
To rival the shading
Of this sadder plot.

Next to your rainbow exclamations
We react like traffic lights, mostly
Telling you to stop –
Despite our own deep-sunk
Unbounded-ness that
Runs free in our hearts,
A long lost mongrel chasing
The red rubber ball of happiness.

Together we pick conkers in the grass
Under the mother chestnuts, thickly armed,
Who stroke and pattern us. But you,
You like the saplings best.

Teenager tree!
Teenager tree!

You run towards them
With arms outstretched
A relay of laughter.

Lank and rustling,
With tickling, yellow leaves,
They are the future
That awaits you, stations

To be touched, arrested by
A shout or shaken by
Your breezy reckoning.

Designs

In the Brazilian jungle, the red
Toenails of passenger 241
Stick out from the forest floor,
The smallest paintings
In God's wide plan.

I see her brushing them,
Carefully, the night before,
The little crimson bristles
Dabbing soft hairs into
The tightest corners.

Passenger 263 tells us
How she chanced upon
The sight, before she set off
For the river, figuring boats
Would bring her rescue –
And she was right. She must,

She mused, have spun,
Like a sycamore wing,
The row of empty seats
Her long stroke of luck.

Ah, the great logic of survival
Opens like Verbrena Melindres,
It's curled buds opening scarlet
Offering six wide-open lips.

The forest gives its explanation
Of the living swell. Frogs and
Crocodiles. The mash and thread
Of a million hung and looping vines
Petals, stiff as horn, falling to the floor.

Butterfly Mine

Quite by chance, and long before
He was widely-known in his own right,
Andy Warhol met Greta Garbo.

In honour of her beauty and her fame
He rushed to give her something
In his name: a drawing of a butterfly.

She took one look at him,
His odd, pale, pitted face,
Screwed up the paper
And threw it to the floor.

But he bent down,
And very carefully
Unfolded the ball.

He took it home that night
And had his mother write, in a careful
Childish script: "Crumpled
Butterfly, By Greta Garbo".

The butterfly was rescued
From the kick of busy feet,
Its urgency unravelling down
A New York street.

As for his mother, Julia, she loved
The brand new tape machine
Her son had given as a gift,
Would sing into the microphone
At night, old Czech folk songs.

She'd play them back,
And sing along
Her harmonies of one,
Lay down on shelves of rhyme
The past and present tense.

Along a hinge of lonely joy,
She'd sing and make
Insinuations of eternity –
Songs that would alight, lopsided
In their flight – as a butterfly.

Stains

Only in a very busy rush
I notice the fat red flower
Has burst. A glance
Gathers the tatters,
Stops me in my tracks
And makes me ask how any
Interruption, needed or
Uncalled for, comes about.

I draw attentions, passing trades,
As much to live by
As a flower – small, side-slung
Ones as much as any other –
But it feels like being called.

Outside the kitchen window
The garden is one big
Fabrication that sets itself up
Against the measurements
Of my own toil and habit.
The summer light
Juggles with shape
Like the pattern of memory,
My arms half lost
In yesterday's plates.

There's a great leafy poetry
To the small tree
That sits outside of me,
Steeped in slow mutation,
Then shivering
In the sudden now.

Armed with fact, it is like
A little god in its own right,
With big broad palms,
Soft, generous clappers,
Amid which, purple berries
Spot the shade.

On the kitchen floor
My daily inattentions to
All that is on offer on the branch
Lie caught and bloodied,
Broken in my stride.

Promises

The bulbs come from the shop
With labels that furnish
Their future glory
In technicolour reds. I take on faith

Their Latin promises
And plant them row by row. Into scenes
Of an ideal summer, my fat seeds
Drop. Perhaps I'll rest

On the comfy lounger
To turn my head from yours
To see these plants rejoice for us.
Love-triangle,

Props of happiness, these bulbs
Are the surest knots
Of expectation. They sit
In my hand, with mad-professor hair,
Wrapped in crispy skins, ready
To wait a full six months
Before taking hold of themselves
And their calm resolution.

I push down
And cover up their fact
With all the longed for pleasures
Of forgetfulness. Then I lie

Down with them,
Four inches down
Beneath the crust,

Out of which all deceptions
Redeem themselves,
Turning into fragrant and
Different-coloured musts.

Display

Amid the conversation of my guests, the lilies
Fill the room with pungent-smelling musk.

Theirs is an orange powdered dust that catches
Every hem and sleeve with bold, paprika kisses.

Surrounded by laughter and a loud conviviality,
They let it all hang out for us, their sexy bits,

Shameless in their quest to seize
The every chance that comes their way. But

It's words, not bees, that dart and fly across the
Perfumed air. And so they contain within them

Circles within circles, an image of our own desire.
I see how the female players, poised and trembling,

Offer up their Ascot hats of pollen, while the boy
Frond stands taller in the middle of his clutch.

How strange it is that his purple, turban-headed tip
Swells up to drip onto the table cloth, a single tear.

How We Met

That night was a strange one, for sure.
Scaramouch was dancing on the rope, the wheelbarrow
Before him with two children and a dog in it: only you
Looked the other way, at the crumbling wall
With flakes of paint that blistered like sores. I could've
Blamed the beer. But there was something else afoot
In the tilt of your gait. And when the man came on
Who could twist himself in knots, your eyes
Landed on me. Despite their skewed direction,
That could have taken in the stars, there was the
Firmest purpose in the look you cast; recklessness,
Conjecture, seriousness, and a weird peace.
You gave a smile I've later seen and seen
And know as yours. Mischief. Swaying on two pegs.
And then, as the room clapped to the act of
The Horse and No Horse, (whose tail stands
Where his head should do), you took me in your arms
And kissed me. Thirty years later,
I can only marvel at it. Yes, that night was strange
For sure. It was the night when the sad man
Who sells the sugared nuts in Covent Garden
Played the silly fool, the one who is at pains
Never to laugh out loud on any other day.

Pox

The year of the pox I was 32.
My face became the moon.
And the only thing I let
You spoon into my mouth
Was the creamy consolation
Of Ambrosia rice pudding.
We'd only just met. But you still
Kissed my cheek, though the flakes
Fell away on their own drift of desire.
The itch was like a coat of burning fire
Especially at night, when tiny
Vesuvia, with green tips, erupted
In the tenderest of creases. And so
I led a life of Caliban, forced to let
You work some magic for a change,
Too sick to grumble or complain
Of being pinch'd to death. Instead
This thing of darkness I acknowledge mine
The lesson of kindness being
That it's better off for being left alone,
Unfettered, clearing the tins from
The side of the bed, the spillages of pills,
Opening curtains into the rank bedroom
That then I called my own. I wear

The scars today like pitted blessings,
That I can touch and wonder at
In the mirror's most terrestrial pond.

Night of the Notorious

A bowl of Twiglets lay
In the centre of the table,
The charred remains
Of little no-bodies. I rose up
From them, to occupy myself,
A little tipsy, but complete,
Licks of salty Marmite still
Clinging to my elbows.

At the bar, the rock chick's eyes
Hung large and wide as moons.
Caroline Aherne walked in
And shouted out, "Courtney, Luv!"
But Courtney didn't get the joke,
So she offered me a chip,
A twinkle in her burning eye.

Sotto voce, the waiter
Told me he was off to be
A rocket scientist. Six years
Of waiting on these tables
Was enough. I tried to joke about
The firmament within my glass
Where little stars did burst,
But he was too intent on
Pouring steady. After that
We all got drunk on the stories
By which we knew one another,
Smoky as kippers.

"Our Trace", turned out to be
the artist Tracey Emin
In two-piece suit, suddenly
Ethereal. She sucked her ciggy
Casting shifty sober eyes
Over the whole clutch of us.

She offered me a line,
Unfolding the wrap not
Four but twenty times.
It was a page from Lorca and the
Line read: *The wounds were
Burning like suns.*

All the taxi driver talked about
On the long ride home
Was the Koran. One truth?
I asked, with liqueur on my breath.
Yes, one truth, he said, spinning
The clapped out vehicle
Through damp deserted streets.

Diva

I made my name
Reaching impossible notes.
When I felt, I always felt it
Right here in my throat. And now
That I am long-gone famous,
What I miss the most?
The way the orchestra tunes-up
A morning chorus
Of baggy human dissonance. The moment
I step into the spot. I always
Trusted that my voice
Was mine, even when the Sphinx
Rested his paws lightly
On my shoulders. Then there was
The five-minute walk from
The hotel to that rehearsal
When I began to seriously wonder.

These days I can laugh
About the trampoline they put
On the other side of the wall
In the last act of my
Difficult Tosca.
Opera takes no hostages.

The flat disc glitters in my hand.
I hear myself travelling
In two directions at once. This is
Me in my prime – the hole
Big enough to stab
A painted nail through.

The Taxidermist's Art

Here comes the bus again
Bringing stops and starts.
Journeys in journeys, that
Time I stood on Essex Road
With glass half-empty on that corner.
It was, I think, an unseasonably warm evening.
I remember my eyes following
The pin-stripes of your suit
As the tracks ran over your hips.
Mostly what I'm left with now
Is the feeling of discomfort as you
Smiled and tilted to me. I refused
Your tacit offerings, half-empty myself,
With sorrows that clung, sticky
As the mottled bubbles of my drink
In slow retreat from thirst. Instead,
I walked down Essex Road,
Away from you, your suit, the chance,
Past a curious shopfront where
A wolf, a cat and cockatoo,
All plump in camaraderie,
Stared forward, glassy-eyed,
Kept alive
By a supplanter's art,
A joker, who had a cheek
To call his musky premises
Get Stuffed. Their eyes still
Search the distance,
Waiting for the call to let them bolt
Out of the door, run clattering
And slipshod, into the road.

Jack Escapes

Three hours was all it took the first time.
He sliced through the ceiling, patiently,
Then lowered himself to the ground
On the rope of his trusty blanket.
Next time, he was pinioned with links.
But he bore through a bar of oak
Nine inches thick, cutting the rings
Of sixty years in sixty hours. While
At liberty, his soft, slim hands dipped
Into the pockets of yet more gentlemen,
So he was thrown into a tiny cell
Where nests of tiny creatures
Nibbled every crevice and darkness
Covered his eyes, blacker than a sack.
When clerics came to visit
He told them they were made of
Gingerbread and that one useful file
Was worth all the Bibles in Christendom.
The final time, they never found out how
He climbed up through a chimney,
Into the Red Room, from there
To the bolted chapel, dropped from
The height of Newgate's topmost rampart
Where the view was good, and the smoky
Shapes of the beyond looked for all the world
Like a city in thrall to its own immutability.
Unable to resist himself, he decided to make
A show of his final arrest: he stole a silver suit,
Hired a fancy coach, and drove back into town
Where the great roar began.

Rule

A millepede crawls
Along a stem: he squeezes
And stretches. He's fat
Then thin. He's a living rule,
An inch of inching. I watch
How his thousand feet
Ripple, a Mexican wave
Moving through a line
Of bristling cadets.
Progress is achieved
By small steps is his
One visible maxim.
Tiny crescents of leaf
Become him. Green worm
On a green background,
An innocent lie.
I put out my finger, but
His blunt face shuns me.
And when I pick him up –
Plump and prickly –
To sit him in my palm,
He twists and oh-so
Fiercely resists,
Un-tying in the air
Myriad sailor's knots.

Glass

I hear a clack
And turn the glass to see it
Cracked in two places,
Across the corner of your smile.

The man in the shop offers
To fix another piece for me,
Three minutes to closing.

Slowly, he slides out a big pane
By its turquoise edges,
Pulling the bigger-than-him rectangle
Carefully from the crowd.
All the time, he uses only
The grip of his fingertips.
Paying due attention to every objection
Within an inch of its life, he swings
The pane, now bowing a little,
Flat onto the work surface.

Through its brittle rubric, I see
His muscles flex and give,
The adroit malleability
That makes all things human
Possible. He runs a score
Down the rule's length.
The glass screams. Then he
Tucks the rule back under the ice,
To snap with measured gentleness
The perfect edge.
No dust flies up from
The hardness. Just absolute
Matter of factness.

I carry my piece of glass back home
Like the cushion under a king's crown,
Watching the sky spit down,
With a mysterious beauty,
Flecks over the sheen.

You smile again,
Under this heaviness,
That could shatter in my hands,
But this time, holds.

Helter Skelter

Atlantic Road,
Average Main Course £12

I eat chunks of venison
And offer no recrimination,
The softest bed of watercress
Slipping at my lips. Outside,
Bananas turn soft and black
Curled in cardboard boxes,
While a train with little lamps
Lit prettily at every window,
Roars to Paris – as though
Love itself were in a rush
And not the waiter who
Presses us to say whether
We need anything else?

Letter from the Lake House

The sound of the pleasure boat
Separates from the water
And comes across to me
As a sign or a message
From myself to myself:
My boat, my pleasure.

Three o'clock and the lake
Is shining brilliantly. I let
Myself flow out and over it
Gathering the distance
With a suck of eye.
My thoughts are quick as swifts,
That fold their wings back
Under these wide eaves. Only

The teapot's bulge embraces me
With ridiculously long and open arms.
Such a dark and swirling eye it sees with.
Ping goes the microwave.
There's always time to stop.

The forest all around here
Is driven through
By a road, by a car.
It arrives at my doorstep
Exhaling the smell of pine needles
Some pirouetting scraps,
A hush softly settling.

I am living in the house
Of the past. You do not need
To worry about not being here.
I am calm as the kettle boils. I find
Myself in the sulky faces of the China cats.
The dance of the jam jars.
A morse of lit and unlit lamps.

The forest is driven through
By a woman who drives a Ford Mondeo
And who is always certain of the
Currency of now. Behind the curtains
I hear her arrive:
Crunch of pebbledash.
Clunk of the door.
Into the house from where I can see
The lake shining like eternity.

The Flats

Today is the day when the old block of flats
Comes down. The police have cordoned off the area.
Men in dark jackets have inspected the alleyways.
A crowd has gathered in the park.
It's due to happen any moment now.
The cameras, on tripods, all point to it.
You must be careful not to blink.
A flare goes up. A puff of smoke
That drifts far right. A thought
Dismissed. And then the
Boom! The windows
Drop their smile.
The walls fall
Soft as eggs.
The spine of the lift shaft is
The last strange doric to topple.
As though all things concrete
Were contingent after all.
A risible horizon.
A laughable offence.
The dust comes then,
Plumping itself slowly from the base,
Bellowing towards us, from a distance,
Then near. Everyone runs, but gets
Caught up in the cloud anyway. Small particles
Of the flats come to rest very gently
In the pleats of my new black jacket.
We all walk out
Of the moment,
Inhaling its musk,
Fond and secret agents now
Of an ongoing dispersal.

Brained-out

I watch t.v. all night, dead-eyed,
Letting the narcotic of strong colour
And loud voices, swim right through me:
Herds of buffalo run across the plain.
A thin lady, with careful hands,
Turns over the skull of our common ancestor.
From a big jar, she fills the cavity,
Letting hundreds of tiny glass balls
Tinkle into the head space.
Later she will count them, one by one,
And make her considered judgement.
There are other important matters. Lucy's pelvis.
The way that when we stand up
We're free to use our hands.
(It took them a while to work that one out.)
And then the sighted workings of the brain.
A man is slowly fed into the machine.
I can see for myself how thought
Looks like a city lit at night.
Memory is a piece of throbbing coral,
Which, like coral, accrues through habit.
Consciousness is the sweep of armies
Engaging and separating across a
Landscape of hills and valleys.
Most of the brain just does its brain thing,
Not noticing. I imagine my own brain
Secretly recognising its sister on the screen –
The bits it can't see for itself –
Like looking at your bum in the shop mirror.
But I also know I have to imagine anything real hard
To make it real. I switch off and go downstairs to bed
Where even as I sleep
The needle scratches my dreams.
The buffalo run across the plain.
The glass balls fall from the jar, and scatter me.

Utopia

I am a tiny man
Living in a house
By Mies van der Rohe.
The walls do not quite hold me.
Instead they pause and gape,
Are wide with longing, lovely views,
Moments to slowly walk through.

Through his generosity I see
The castle on the hill top
Is perfectly orientated,
As though it was built for me alone.
If all sights could be seen just so!
Every half-brick is accounted for
And I am always being pointed
Towards one beauty or another:
Pebbles in the pool,
A tree's reflection in the polish,
Marble like the very map of heaven.

Mostly, though, I'm left to do a lot of thinking.
It's very calm for miles around. The stream
Runs down the mountain, under the bridge,
Carrying all passion away on it.
Away it flees, into the grainy tone
Of a thirties German village
Where tall black boots
Have only just begun

To march. I sit at the grand piano,
Lay my fingers over the ivories
Touching their coolnesses.
I wonder what it means

To break from this position
Into a song, what anyone would need
To make a form for their escape,
What wings are safe to fly on?

Gazebo

At the bottom of the garden
Sits the summer house you built:
Husband Zen
A ten foot tall
Glass octagon
That the cats creep inside
To piss. We light
A big fat joint whose
Acrid smoke will slowly
Defy the stench
And odd geometry
That surround us.
It's quiet in here.
Windless. I suck
And hear the crackle
Of paper and tobacco
Burning tips.
The relief of a little silence
Then between us.
Mint in the borders.
The defeated football on the lawn,
The backs of the houses with their windows
Full of yellow light.

You explain how you dug
The trenches first,
Then slotted in the panes.
The wooden roof is
The hat of a Chinese mandarin
Securing atop.
The equation pi
Came into the plan
Then out of your head
So here it stands.
Pi in action. Pi vindicated.
And to crown the victory

Some light refreshment
Ruled by another universal law
Evidenced in breaking point,
Specific, percussive,
The drizzle's most
Tender applause.

The Visitor

after Fra Angelico

I have a visitor – who comes
Before she came, like a premonition –
Who enters the open doorway
Of my solitude, stepping right into
My haven. The buttercups
Are unimpressed, her footfalls
Are so light: the fauna acts as
Innocent as usual. But I see her:
Bright, clear, meticulous,
Almost in the mirror of myself,
But so much better. Solicitous
In her announcement, she arrives
Like the gaze of someone
Who has loved me from afar
For a long, long time,
I did not realise.
Such rosey drapes.
Her pleatedness gathers me
In swags of grace,
Her expectation and her knowingness.
I am more than ever simply me
In this otherness she brings me,
This quiet loveliness
That touches
With coloured feathers,
Fantastic wings. Soon
We will exchange our gifts of words.
But only this moment, I have
Just looked up, out of
The hood of myself. Here
Is the brightest thing,
morning on her cheek,
Not embarrassed after all,
But glorious.

Bone and Butter

after Joseph Beuys

These two slim reindeer skulls,
Are like bicycle seats also,
But without Picasso's ribald
Sense of humour. Sockets

Where their eyes once saw
Are scoops now big enough
For billiard balls. Along

Comes a man
In a trilby hat who spoons
Into the brain place
A pound of butter.

It makes death look
A little delicious and gives
The twin ghost animals
Something to think about.

Two dots over the vowel
Make a moo an ooh. It's
The reindeer mating call.
The butterman pretends

To be a reindeer now.
He forks his fingers in the air
Like antlers, or an insult,
Or thought itself, as
Into the skull's bare pathways
The butter weeps.

Herders

In the coldest spot on earth
Temperatures drop as low
As minus forty. The men
Wear thick reindeer fur
As they chase the reindeer
Over the ice. They eat only
Reindeer meat to keep them
Warm. Nothing that isn't necesssary
Survives. As the reindeer run,
There's a fog of breath and braying
That curls into the forest.
The clacking antlers
Echo the shapes of the trees,
The forked branch,
Furred with snow.
When night falls, the stove
Is a godhead to be fed
With wood and circled
With laughter. Under rugs
Of thickest reindeer hide,
The men think of their
Women back at home,
Those tender slopes.
They urge their single
Stalks of longing to
Conclusion and the
Sweetest sleep. Dawn
Comes up from behind
The dark mountain, to touch
Them with a deep blue kiss.

Staigue Fort

How they stacked the wall,
Stone by uncemented stone,
To angle the tilting incline
With such precision,
We don't know. But
There's a solid satisfaction
To be had from the pattern,
Mounting the steps as they did
In the shape of an X,
On the inside ring,
The just right trot
From foot to foot
To the top of the rampart.

From here they could view the sea and
Live on this bleak seat from where,
Through a theatre of rain and wind and admonishment,
They could sit and watch the coming of
The thing that frightened them the most.

Plumbline

Silence falls through me
Like a weight through water.

The water is a choppy sea,
Wide as experience. But

Silence falls through me
In a vertical to test

The forces of forgetting
With a strict adherence

To the here and now.
It's difficult to tell just

How, and by what chaste
Method, it does its work of

Wiping down the frontages
Of agency and choice. But

Wild flowers of wisdom
Grow here on the walls

And look to be nearly
Within picking distance.

Petals blush against
The weight of this silence

As it visits and passes them,
Like an old gardener

With kind hands. There
Is no earth, beyond earth,

No landing floor. Only more
Loaded gentleness, that

Speechlessly pours and turns
In this, my curious element.

Smoothly

On effortless summer days, waves
Break easeful on the sand and we pick up
Pebbles that sit
Smoothly in the hand, to ponder.
Each one, when turned,
Is utterly unique, although
They also look, en masse, to be competing

For a single perfection. This beach's lot are
Quartz-shot, ribbed and knobbly,
And touch each other
Sparingly, abandoned
To single particulars and
Random angles of contact.

When my hand falls
On the feel of something smooth
I think of music or of God,
Writes Saint Augustine.
Between the pages of the book
That pertain to the ethics
Of beauty and suffering,
The sand makes a home.

The ground-down parts
That you and I
Let slip between us,
Trickle back
In winter, in bed,
Onto my bare belly,
The gentlest little avalanche.

Walking in Redwoods

Into the wood where the trees are very tall
There is no noise. The greatest ambition
Granted to a tree is here advantaged,
Lean and single-minded every one.
What occupies – slowly, formidably –
Is the pushing up together to the sky:
The vertical and horizontal will pay
Each other's due, a price arrived at
Through the loaded agency of tree.

In the middle of the oldest trunk
The sapling ghosts a presence
Locked amongst the perfumed rooms
Of its children's children. (The birth
Of Christ is just another orbit in the rings.)
Their own purpose is their only cause: conscience
Before conscience could touch itself.

We look to one another in this place.
Our laughter's fleet as birds
The praise we try to put in words
That fails us. It's as though we never
Really walked through here at all. Even before
We rolled down the thickness of our socks
– to rub our aching calves –
The generous shade will have gathered us.

Sticks

I use my crutches
For theatrical effect, it's true.
The lady from the church
Who said that I was fibbing,
She was right. But I find that
Folk prefer to see the sight of me
As something they'd expect,
As someone who deserves them –
They don't mind which – either
When nothing's offered
Or a penny's proffered.
Cause and effect is
My business and my art.
It's on the fur of my tongue.
It's in the milk of my eye.
The leap to attention
In the heart of the conscience
Or its slacker opposite. I know
Just how the passing glances
Hold me, like an image
Of catastrophe, their furthest selves.
I try to comfort them
With my own prop of sympathy,
My helping hands of wood.
It's like a welcome echo really,
The issue understood. I'm cheeky
As a lie and almost cheerful.
So much so, that sometimes even I
Can barely see the person who doesn't
Need his sticks, the one who wouldn't
Need their trickery,
To run, run away.

On Brownswood Road

The girl on Brownswood Road
Is all fake fur, with spikey snags,
That blur her fuzzy edges even more.
You can see her any time of day.
Slightly exaggerating. Not too much,
But enough. Like it's film noir,
Not Brownswood Road,
She's trading on. Two policemen
Approach her from the corner.
One holds his hand oddly
Underneath his jacket.
Passing the garage, a mechanic
Points his fingers like a gun.
He's jigging to the music.
His mate makes the sound of a shot,
Then smiles at me with flashing teeth.
Even the little girl in the pram,
Is casting her child eyes over
To the other side of the road as though
Something is about to happen....
It's four o'clock in the afternoon.
A diagram could explain it: arrows,
Flow charts, lines of supply.
The trees shake down suspicion.
A bus changes gear. Suddenly
The radio is chatty and loud.

Props

The drop-handle racer
Stands there for itself
On a little swung down leg.
But right now, it's also
Bigger than just that –
Adolescence itself, clanky,
Thin-limbed, dumb –
That tiptoe touching
Of the floor to come.

The old lawnmower too,
With switches dead and slack,
You can smell the goodness of the grass
That it has cut and run, like it could
Level every loneliness
Or desecrate the peace,
You don't know which.

The boy is slumped
And crying on the floor.
He wraps his arm around his face
To hide the thing both true and terrible.
He is in the moment, given-up,
As none of us quite know
When time will come to us
Arriving now, electric,
Through the rising door.

We watch him – from the driveway
With the headlights on – to wonder
Whatever it could be, what loss or gain
Or hard exchange,
He'd cry like that for.

The Guard

Only water measures me
In blue and blameless lassitude.
I am happy being shallow
In the deep end, chinning
The waterline. I try

To let it help me –
My guide and encourager,
Licker of lights – but all
The deeds of the day
Follow me. I push aside

Everything that lies
Ahead of me. All
My washings-off
Meet the hardness of the edge
At angles commensurate
To all that I spend. But suppleness
Within the hour
Eludes me. Climbing out I pass

The boy who watches from the tower.
He leans his head and gazes
At the place he'd rather be.
In the pocket of his track suit
His walkie-talkie
Crunches and splutters
With all the tired urgency
Of other people's trouble.

Twice

It's been a day of storms today.
The thunder and the lightning won't stop.
Front page news: an Italian doctor
Wants to be the first man ever
To make from the genes of a mother,
A child. Behind the doctor, a wall of photos,
A shoal of embryos, dainty as sea horses.
These babies in-the-making
Sit at his left shoulder
And arrive out of themselves
Into a promised future. The doctor
Is speaking at a press conference.
The embryos are in the background.
Enlarged a hundred times,
They seem curiously not ours:
Impossibly tender,
Distantly-related,
Peeled langoustines.
They sleep inside themselves,
On the cusp of becoming,
And pray intently with lidless,
Sightless eyes. What we imagine
Is already on the way to coming true.
Images of embryos
Float in my mind
As I expand my line of argument,
Pale and translucent,
Intricate and water-logged.
Frog spawn brains
Quiver in thimble-sized,
Wafer-thin craniums. Outside,
Bolts of lighting prick the city:
Random acts, specifically discharged,
And still a little frightening.

The Far-off Field

In possession of the freedom
Afforded by silence,
The mildness of its hunger,
I take a walk
Along the riverbank.
Two swans are swimming –
So I stop before I start
To watch the ribbons
Of their wakes criss
Cross. Then on and past
A tree trunk, hollowed-out,
A wizened place to peer at.
Through the gate,
A little nervously I go,
Where a bull sits
Square amongst his clan,
The skin of his huge neck
Gathered round him, thick
As heavy curtains. I survive
The measure of his eye,
Cross over the bridge, see
The vivid colour of the sky
Ride on the river's surface,
Reflecting like lovers,
One held in the other. Then
Past couples in the real,
Who talk loudly and in hand –
Their dogs and children
Running on ahead of them –
To reach the far-off field
Where cream cows stand.

The moment draws
To its fullest height, before
I turn around – my inwardness
Thrown out before me now –
In the shape of my shadow,
Through the coming folds of night,
Re-capturing. Delivered.

Parallel

Our empty sleeves,
Mine and yours both,
Proffer midnight.
Sparrows,
With delicate gold feathers,
Are imbedded
In the lacquer
Of the black Japanese box.
Its doors will not quite close.
They slip the clasp, while
Bracelets snake on top
And gather dust.
Outside the frost is bitter,
And sparkles in the cracks.
My comb. Your ring. The scarf
You gave me in the summer
In a pavement café. I watch
Its pattern turn
A dozen hairpin corners
All in pink.
Our processional selves
March into January
Smelling only
Vaguely of us now.
Buddha sits cross-legged
Very calm,
On the postcard
From Thailand.
He's jammed
Between the frame
And the mirror's dusty sheen
Where time doubles.
Behind his lids
Sunlight flickers
On the other side
Of the world.

Blind

Woken up, now here we are
Both reading books in bed.
We are two shoots growing
From the same fat bulb, or
Two bright candles, feeding
On the wicks of written words.
Now and again,
Your toes brush mine
As you read a funny line
That tickles you, setting
In motion an oblique
Yet companionable
Chain of related events.
There are workmen outside
Who shout and whistle
Loudly in the street,
Whose faces pass across
The sun-lit blind like
Shadow puppets.
Their brisk gaits swoon
In front of us, are busy
Loading bricks. Going
Back and forth, they
Make a pattern of the
Bedroom's hooded light.
But safely veiled and
Firmly out of sight,
What we mostly do
Is hear them – noise
That our minds can skip across
On stepping stones of silence,
Luxurious and unaware,
Making no sense at all of
Their strange dark music,
Nor feeling any need to even try.

The Wonder

The girl won't stop running –
Sprinting towards the Great Pyramid.
It squats in front of her – a picture
Of itself – grown large enough
For capture. She runs in the sandy
Gutter in slip-ons and a pencil skirt.
Didn't she guess she'd arrive here
One of these days? The way she
Skittles along, she could be six
Again, a childish scamp next
To the plod of the serious camel.
It's hot too, her ponytail is pulling
At her scalp. She's damp with
Swept back tension. Turning
A bend in the road, a sign reads:
BEHOLD THE FOUR SIDED MOUNTAIN.
I follow her along the final curl and
See into the heart of the zombie monument.
Back here in her slipstream, I become
An echo of her longing. I see too clearly
What will happen. I try to warn her.
But she runs on, into the wonder ahead.

The Spare Room

Sun, through the widest window,
Pools onto the floor. A spider
On the hedge outside, sits bang
Centre in the middle of his world,
Which lights up, silver and precarious.
Blowy October. The book read,
And the flank of my cheek, alight.
I think of that box room we had,
Bent around a corner, the little
Single bed we kept there, impossible
To fit into the jaws of angles planned
By way of cheap conversion:
Every side, the wrong side. I spent
An afternoon in there, clearing out junk,
Pushing the mattress around, then tying
The knots of four big plastic bags
That sat with me in a path of light, the window
Marking me with its side-slung cross
As someone who was spoken for.
I remember quite clearly how the
Shapes of leaves ran over the spread,
Taking long bows in the breeze.

The important guest I made the bed for
Never came. But the little lamp looked pretty anyway,
We thought, looking in on the scene before turning in.
That room swims through me now, like a fish,
The filligree of my finger whorls tapping
Four o'clock in the afternoon, exactly.

Old Man on a Perilous Bridge

after Hokusai

Crossing the suspension bridge
Between the provinces
Of Hida and Etchu,
We have to tread
On little wooden slats
That take the slack over
The deepest canyon. You, me,
Chancing these ropes,
And those three birds
Riding an updraught. Below
Spruces pierce the air
With perfumed finials,
And I spy, on the other bank,
Two deer grazing the slope
One casting us a quick,
Disinterested glance now.
This load on my back is full
Of the hugging heat of a long journey.
Steady as you go. Don't test it!
See left, how the blue mountain
Has unconquerable presence,
And points as might
The finger of a philosopher,
Towards tall, elaborate certainties.
Ignore the sheer ledge that
Sprouts a dotted coat
Of close-companioned weeds.
Breathe in. From here

The ground is the lid of a dream
And all that can be compassed, breaks through.
We cross over on a ladder of indigo. Hokusai
Told us to ponder our surroundings
Very carefully, three quarters of the way over,
Although swinging in the air
Between Hida and Etchu,
He'll admit – when pushed –
That he never visited either.

The Collection

The men have come for the rubbish.
The neighbours have tied it up with string.
It's raining. And the slimy wood
Falls over itself
In loose bundles
Under their arms.
They pick up the stinking sticks of furniture
Wearing vivid green bibs and
Rubber gloves, wide-pawed as grizzlies.
They are crunching down the refuse with their boots.
The skinny dark one brings it to the back.
The square fat one packs it in, carefully as treasure.
They call to each other
With the strong voices of men at sea.
Everyone else is busy in an office or tending a baby.
You can hear the patina of the drizzle,
The waft and weft of the silence settling after them.
The streets offer them a surfeit of unwantedness.
They drive off laughing together,
The muck of the world in the back of the van.

Movements

All I've read about today
Is art: the Abstract Expressionists.
The seriousness of their scene.
The all-over-ness of their canvases.

At four o'clock
I catch the last light in the park and
Let my concentration run amok
In piles of leaves: their gestures

Have not yet become a parody.
They spin as they fall
According to form.
Then lie on top of one another
With a random sense of design.

Curls of the palest yellow
Collect around the bottom of a tree –
Like an idea in which no-one
Can any longer believe.
All shaken down.

Clement Greenberg
Defrocked of virtue
Holds up the sky no more.

Patterns congregate in the dark.
All the black branches are up
To the task of imperceptibly
Letting go.

Acknowledgements

Acknowledgements are due to the editors of the following publications where some of these poems first appeared: *Poetry Wales,* and *Boomerang.* 'Pox' was one of the winners of the 2001 New Forest Open Poetry Competition, judged by Matthew Sweeney. 'Night of the Notorious' and 'The Taxidermist's Art' were broadcast on BBC Radio Wales in 2001 in *A Sense of Place.*

Big thanks to Neil Rollinson for all his encouragement and for his appraisal of the manuscript. Thanks also to my editor Amy Wack for all her attentions. Thanks to Binnie for her loan of Kiwi the dog and my brother Alan for taking the photograph for the cover. Last on the list, but first in my heart, thank you Rachael.